The Adventures of Scuba Jack
Copyright 2021 by Beth Costanzo
All rights reserved

Meerkats live in the deserts and grasslands off the southern tip of Africa. They are cute, bushy animals, with brown-striped fur and large eyes that have dark patches around them. They are 20 inches tall, including their tail, and weigh up to 2.2 pounds! A group of meerkats is called a mob.

These animals are extremely social and live together in burrows. They dig the burrows with their long, sharp claws. Their burrows are underground to keep them safe from predators, like snakes, hawks and eagles, and these burrows protect them from the hot sun. Burrows can be 16 feet long! A group of meerkats will use up to five different burrows at a time.

Every morning, the mob leaves the burrow and starts to look for food. They use their great sense of smell to look for spiders, scorpions, beetles, and caterpillars. They will also eat eggs, fruit, birds, and small reptiles. Back at the burrow, other meerkats stay behind to babysit the baby meerkats, called pups.

While they are looking for food, a meerkat, called a sentry, will keep an eye out for predators. If they sense danger they will let out a high-pitched squeal. The mob will hide in safe places called bolt-holes during an emergency. If they are caught, they will try to look vicious by showing their teeth and claws.

MEERKATS QUIZ

QUIZ

Write the correct answer in the box

Where do meerkats live?

1- Caves

2- Trees

3- Burrows

QUIZ

Write the correct answer in the box

Who is on lookout for predators?

1- A sentry

2- Pups

3- Predators

QUIZ

Write the correct answer in the box

If meerkats get caught by a predator, they will try to look fierce by showing their _____?

1- Nose

2- Teeth and claws

3- Eyes

QUIZ

Write the correct answer in the box

Baby Meerkats are called ____

1- Pups

2- Cubs

3- Kats

MEERKATS ACTIVITIES

Trace then rewrite the phrase below.

M for Meerkat

Count the meerkats then circle the answer.

9   7   8    5   6   7

7   6   8    7   9   8

Maze

Help the Meerkat to find its way

MEERKATS CRAFT

Meerkat Craft

1- Cut out the Meerkat Parts
2- Glue the head to the body
3- Glue one hand to the front of the body and one hand to the back of the body
4- Glue one leg to the front of the body and one leg to back of the body
5- Glue the tail to the back of the body
6- Color the Meerkat!

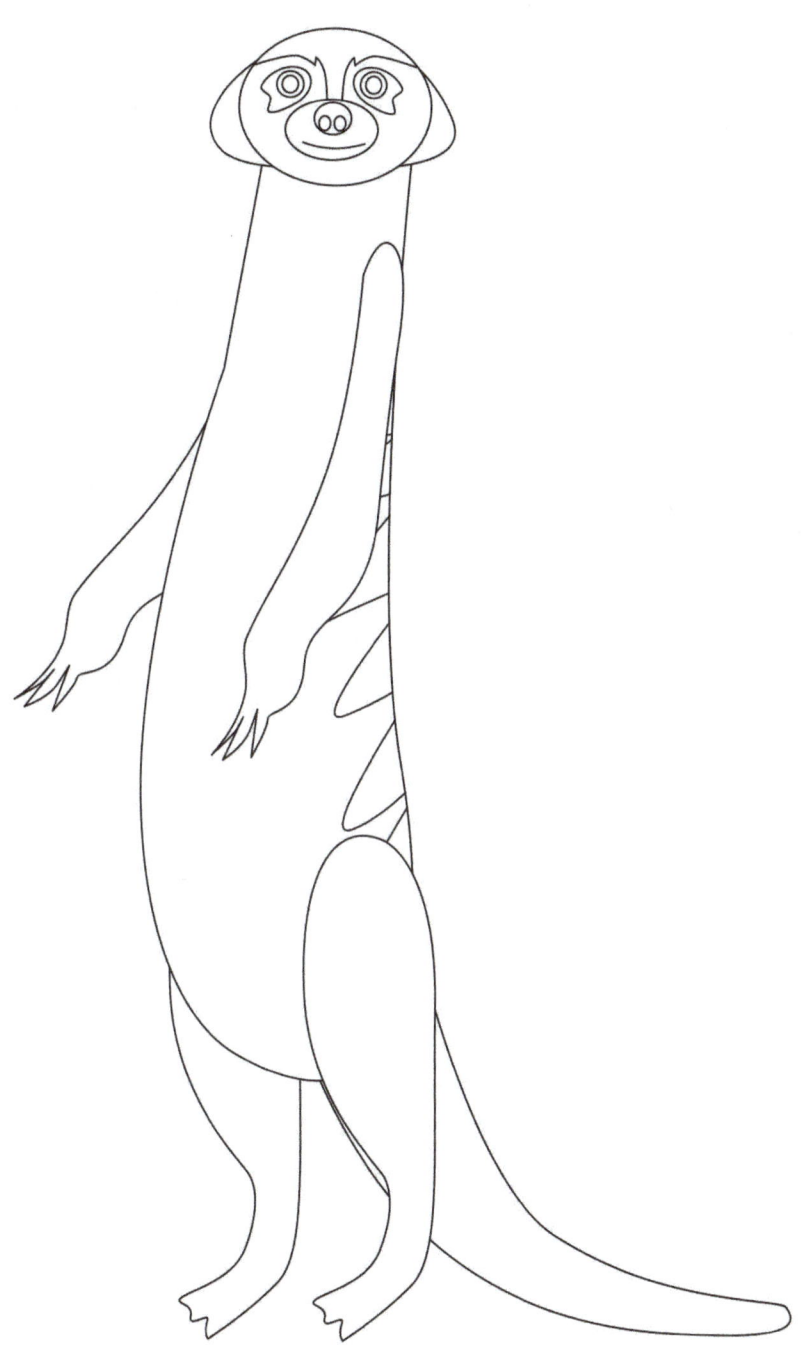

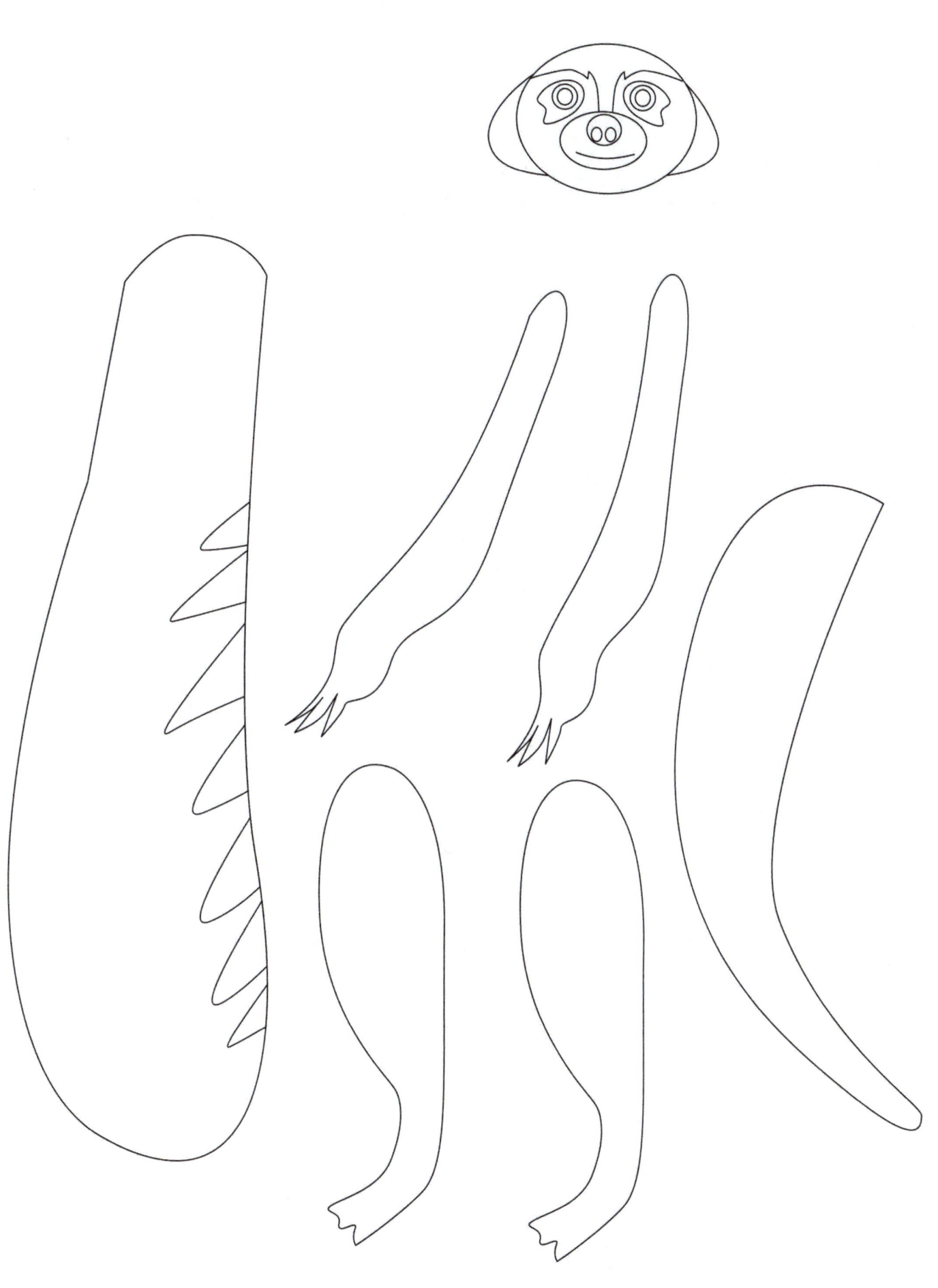

Visit us at:

www.adventuresofscubajack.com

www.ingramcontent.com/pod-product-compliance
Lightning Source LLC
Chambersburg PA
CBHW060429010526
44118CB00017B/2426